The Spelt Bakers Pan Loaves

by

Janet Féirín

Arán Foods Inc.

www.thespeltbakers.ca

The Spelt Bakers Pan Loaves
Text copyright Aran Foods Inc.
Photos copyright 2011 Aran Foods Inc.

No part of this publication may be reproduced, sorted in a retrieval system or transmitted, in any form or by any means, without prior written permission of the author or publisher.

Library and Archives Canada Cataloguing in Publication

Feirin, Janet, 1967 –
   The Spelt Bakers Pan Loaves/Janet Feirin ; photographer, Christine Hedbaut

ISBN 978-0-9736624-1-2

Design & Production: Aran Foods Inc.
Photography: Aran Foods Inc.

Published by Aran Foods Inc.

To all the Spelties,
Enjoy your sandwiches!

Contents

Introduction 5

About Spelt 6

Bread Baking Directions 7

Pan Loaf Recipes

    Integral Bread 18

    Omega-Protein Bread 20

    Spelt & Spuds (White Potato Bread) 22

    Seedy Spelt & Spuds (Multigrain) Bread 24

    Raisin-Cinnamon & Spuds Bread 26

    Spelt Berry Bread 28

    Spelt Brown Honey Bread 30

    White Spelt Bread 32

Miscellaneous

    Cooked Spelt Berries 34

    Potato Mush 35

    Tools & Equipment 36

Introduction

I have been baking with Spelt since the early 1990's and opened Aran Foods Inc. "Vancouver's Original Spelt Bakery" in 1998. After 12 years of baking professionally, the number and variety of recipes that were developed are extensive.

In this book you will find a step by step instruction guide on how to make the eight most popular breads from Aran Foods Inc. modified to be made in a home kitchen.

I highly recommend purchasing a Kitchen Aid Mixer to be able to quickly and easily mix the breads, top quality bread pans and an oven thermometer. I have found that the biggest difficulties in making bread at home has been getting the right temperatures and having the right tools.

Whether you use this book to make the one favourite over and over again or make all eight breads on a regular basis, I hope you enjoy the process of baking and the smell of fresh bread at home the way I have enjoyed the smell at the bakery.

For more recipes and books, find us at
www.thespeltbakers.ca

Thank you,

Janet Feirin,

President

Aran Foods Inc.

About Spelt

Spelt is a grain that was cultivated thousands of years ago and became widespread in central Europe during the Bronze Age, becoming very popular in Southern Germany and Switzerland during the Iron Age, making it's way to southern Britain by 500 B.C.

In terms of baking with Spelt, there is a different water solubility and the flour does not have additives that help stabilize the baking process. What I have found baking with Spelt is that the adjustments that I have made are marginal and yet make all the difference between a heavy loaf of bread and a nice light fluffy loaf of bread.

In this book, I have endeavored to write the recipes so that all of the timing is available to you as well as photos so that you are able to see what it looks like at each stage of the making, rising and baking process.

It has been said that Spelt is suitable for "some" baking as it does contain gluten but it is a moderate amount of gluten. I have developed recipes for all sorts of products with Spelt including croissants and pasta.

Environmentally, Spelt also has its benefits. It is a low yielding crop that does not take as many nutrients from the soil and therefore is a more sustainable crop long term. It also thrives without the application of fertilizers and is resistant to frost and other extreme weather conditions. The thick husk protects it from pollutants and insects making it a fantastic option in the organic farming industry.

Nutritionally Spelt contains carbohydrates, protein, fat, dietary minerals and vitamins, all of which we would expect. The interesting part about Spelt is the amino acids that it contains within the protein. There are 9 essential amino acids that our bodies need to obtain from our food and all of them are available in Spelt.

I believe that Spelt is a wonder grain that is good for people and the planet we live on. Together we can change the world, one loaf of bread at a time.

Janet Féirín

❦ Bread Baking Directions ❦

Spelt Bread - in 12 Steps

All the bread recipes in this book can be made by following our simple 12 step process.

❦ 1 ❦   Gather Ingredients & Equipment

Each recipe details the ingredients needed. Lay them out to ensure you have everything on hand before you begin. The recipes start on page X. Gather your equipment and make sure everything is clean and dry. All equipment can be purchased from a good kitchen supply store. If you do not already own a Kitchen Aid stand mixer, we highly recommend purchasing one or its' equivalent. Several different stores have them on sale periodically throughout the year. It is an investment you should seriously consider.

Equipment:
• A Kitchen Aid stand mixer.
• 2 x 1 lb. bread pans.
• Counter plastic scraper.
• A metal dough divider/scraper.
• Measuring spoons.
• 4 cup measure.
• Brush for oiling your bread pans.
• Counter space for shaping & kneading.
• Cooling rack to let baked bread cool.

✣ 2 ✣   Mixing Dough

Place all ingredients in recipe into the Kitchen Aid mixing bowl in the order listed in the recipe. Put on dough hook and mix on low — speed #1 — for 3 minutes.

✣ 3 ✣   Scrape & Continue Mixing

Now, scrape the dough from the sides of the bowl, leaving the dough in the bowl. Then, continue mixing dough, on medium low — speed № 2, for an additional 5 minutes.

✐ 4 ✐ First Rising

A. Remove the dough hook

B. Rub a bit of vegetable oil on top of dough. This will prevent the plastic / cling wrap from sticking to the dough

C. Cover with plastic / cling wrap

D. Leave on your counter, covered and let rise, for 40 minutes, until double in size.

✐ 5 ✐ Punch Down Dough, Second Rising

Punch down the dough and let rise again, covered as before, for 30 minutes.

✤ 6 ✤   Divide into Two Loaves

Sprinkle some spelt flour onto an area of your countertop approximately the size of a dinner plate. Use the plastic dough scraper to take the dough out of the bowl and put it onto the area and shape into a big ball. Separate in 2 equal parts, (approximately 750 g each, if you have a scale). The metal dough divider is designed for this purpose but a sharp chef's knife will work.

✥ 7 ✥   Shape into 2 Balls

Shape into 2 balls, having enough flour on the counter so the dough does not stick to the counter. You can shape the balls with one hand against the counter or with two hands. Be gentle and check to make sure there isn't any tearing in the dough.

✥ 8 ✥   Gently Flatten

Gently flatten each of the balls with the palm of your hands to get rid of any air pockets. Sprinkle a bit more flour on your counter if the dough begins to stick.

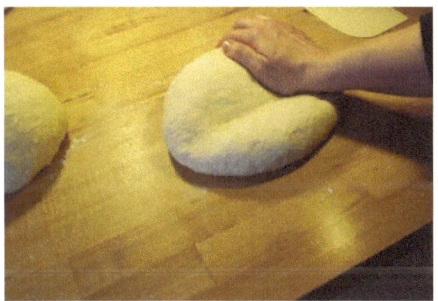

℘ 9 ℘ Shape into Logs

Shape & roll into a log shape to fit your bread pan.

a. Start by making a shallow crest in the middle.

b. Fold the dough lengthwise.

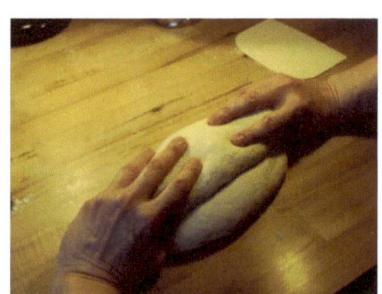

c. Press gently to seal.

d. Roll again to form a log.

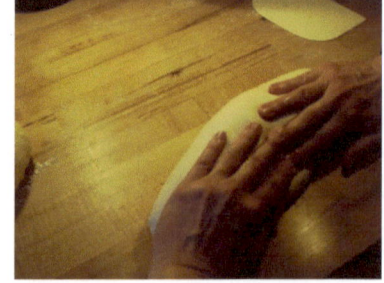

e. Ready to rise.

✎ 10 ✎ Place in Pan, Third Rising

Use a quality oil or butter and oil your bread pans using the brush. Place your bread in you're the oiled bread pan. Gently oil the top of the loaves, cover with plastic / cling wrap and let rise again until double in size – approximately 30 minutes.

❦ 11 ❦ Bake

Preheat the oven to 375° F.

Remove the saran wrap gently and bake in pre-heated oven, on the middle rack, for 10 to 15 minutes. Spray the loaves lightly with a water bottle filled with warm water. Continue baking for another 10 minutes until the loaves are lightly golden on the top and bottom.

℘12℘ Cool & Enjoy!

Remove the bread gently from the pan. Make sure that the sides are not stuck to the pan or else the bread will rip as you try to remove it from the loaf pan. Cool the bread on a cooling rack for at least 15 minutes before slicing and/or freezing.

Personal Notes

Pan Loaf Recipes

Integral Bread 18

Omega-Protein Bread 20

Spelt & Spuds (White Potato Bread) 22

Seedy Spelt & Spuds (Multigrain) Bread 24

Raisin-Cinnamon & Spuds Bread 26

Spelt Berry Bread 28

Spelt Brown Honey Bread 30

White Spelt Bread 32

ꕤInteg ralꕤ

Integral Bread

American	Ingredients	Metric	Imperial
2 1/2 cups	hot water, not boliing	600 ml	20 0z
2 tbsp.	vegetable oil, any kind	30 ml	2 tbsp.
3 tbsp.	blackstrap molasses	45 ml	3 tbsp.
2 tsp.	sea salt	2 tsp.	2 tsp.
2 tsp.	organic cane sugar	2 tsp.	2 tsp.
1/3 cup	cooked spelt berries	50 g	2 oz.
4 1/4 cups	white spelt flour	540 g	1 lb. 3 oz.
2 cups	whole spelt flour	280 g	10 oz.
1 tbsp.	quick active dry yeast	1 tbsp.	1 tbsp.
	seed mix		
2/3 cup	sunflower seeds	100g	4 oz.
1/3 cup	sesame seeds	50 g	2 oz.
1/3 cup	pumpkin seeds	40 g	1 1/2 oz.
1/2 cup	flax meal (ground flax seeds)	70 g	3 oz.

Follow the 12-step instructions.

Preheat oven to 350° F.

Note:
Reserve 2 tablespoons of seed mix for the topping and sprinkle on top of the bread just prior to baking.

Integral Bread - Nutrition Facts (per 45g):

Calories: 100; Total Fat: 2g; Saturated Fat: .2g; Cholesterol: 0mg; Sodium: 120mg; Carbohydrates: 20g; Fibre: 2g; Sugars 1g; Protein: 4g;

Omega-Protein Bread

Omega-Protein Bread

American	Ingredients	Metric	Imperial
	flax mixture, see method below		
1/3 cup	flax seeds	60 g	2 oz.
2/3 cup	cold water	160 ml	6 oz.
1/4 cup	vegetable oil	60 ml	2 oz.
2 cups	hot water, not boiling	500 ml	16 oz.
3 tbsp.	organic cane sugar	50 g	3 tbsp.
2 tsp.	sea salt	2 tsp.	2 tsp.
7 1/2 cups	white spelt flour	940 g	2 lb. 1 oz.
1 tbsp.	quick active dry yeast	1 tbsp.	1 tbsp.

Follow the 12-step instructions.

Preheat oven to 350° F.

Flax Mixture:

mix the flax and cold water in a food processor and after 3 minutes, slowly add oil while mixing. Place in bottom of mixer bowl and add remaining ingredients.

Omega Protein Bread - Nutrition Facts (per 45g):

Calories: 100; Total Fat: 2g; Saturated Fat: .1g; Cholesterol: 0mg; Sodium: 95mg; Carbohydrates: 20g; Fibre: 2g; Sugars 1g; Protein: 4g;

Spelt & Spuds Bread

White Potato Bread

Spelt & Spuds Bread

White Potato Bread

American	Ingredients	Metric	Imperial
2/3 cup	potato mush, page 35	150 g	5 oz.
1 3/4 cup	hot water, not boiling	415 ml	14 oz.
3 tbsp.	organic cane sugar	50 g	3 tbsp.
2 tbsp.	vegetable oil	30 ml	2 tbsp.
2 tsp.	sea salt	2 tsp.	2 tsp.
7 1/2 cups	white spelt flour	940 g	2 lb. 1 oz.
1 tbsp.	quick active dry yeast	1 tbsp.	1 tbsp.

Follow the 12-step instructions.

Preheat oven to 350° F.

Spelt and Spuds - Nutrition Facts (per 45g):

Calories: 100; Total Fat: 1g; Saturated Fat: 0g; Cholesterol: 0mg; Sodium: 95mg; Carbohydrates: 17g; Fibre: 2g; Sugars 1g; Protein: 4g;

Seedy Spelt & Spuds Bread

Multigrain Bread

❧Seedy Spelt & Spuds Bread☙

Multigrain Bread

American	Ingredients	Metric	Imperial
2/3 cup	potato mush, page 35	150 g	5 oz.
1 3/4 cup	hot water, not boiling	415 ml	14 oz.
3 tbsp.	organic cane sugar	50 g	3 tbsp.
2 tbsp.	vegetable oil	30 ml	2 tbsp.
2 tsp.	sea salt	2 tsp.	2 tsp.
4 1/2 cups	white spelt flour	600 g	1 lb. 5 oz.
2 cups	whole spelt flour	280 g	10 oz.
1/4 cup	quick oats	30 g	1 oz.
3 tbsp.	spelt flakes	30 g	1 oz.
2 tbsp.	sunflower seeds	20 g	2 tbsp.
2 tbsp.	flax meal, ground flax seeds	20 g	2 tbsp.
1 tbsp.	millet	10 g	1 tbsp.
1 tsp.	sesame seeds	5 g	1 tsp.
1 tbsp.	quick active dry yeast	11 g	1 tbsp.

Follow the 12-step instructions.

Preheat oven to 350° F.

Seedy Spelt and Spuds - Nutrition Facts (per 45g):

Calories: 100; Total Fat: 2g; Saturated Fat: 0g; Cholesterol: 0mg; Sodium: 95mg; Carbohydrates: 17g; Fibre: 3g; Sugars 1g; Protein: 4g;

Raisin-Cinnamon & Spuds Bread

Raisin-Cinnamon & Spuds Bread

American	Ingredients	Metric	Imperial
1 1/3 cups	sultana raisins, soaked, see below	220 g	8 oz.
2/3 cup	potato mush, page 35	150 g	5 oz.
1 3/4 cup	hot water, not boiling	415 ml	14 oz.
3 tbsp.	organic cane sugar	50 g	3 tbsp.
2 tbsp.	vegetable oil	30 ml	2 tbsp.
2 tsp.	sea salt	2 tsp.	2 tsp.
7 2/3 cups	white spelt flour	930 g	2 lb.
2 tsp.	ground cinnamon	2 tsp.	2 tsp.
1/8 tsp.	ground cardamom	1/8 tsp.	1/8 tsp.
1 tbsp.	quick active dry yeast	11 g	1 tbsp.

Follow the 12-step instructions.

Pour boiling water over sultanas and soak for 5 minutes. Drain as much water as you can before putting in mixer, then add remaining ingredients in order listed.

Preheat oven to 350° F.

Spelt Raisin-Cinnamon & Spuds Bread - Nutrition Facts (per 45g):
Calories: 115; Total Fat: 1g; Saturated Fat: 0g; Cholesterol: 0mg; Sodium: 130mg; Carbohydrates: 26g; Fibre: 2g; Sugars 6g; Protein: 4g;

❧Spelt Berry Bread❦

Spelt Berry Bread

American	Ingredients	Metric	Imperial
2 1/2 cups	hot water, not boiling	600 ml	20 oz.
3 tbsp.	honey	45 ml	3 tbsp.
2 tbsp.	vegetable oil	30 ml	2 tbsp.
2 tsp.	sea salt	2 tsp.	2 tsp.
5 cups	white spelt flour	640 g	1 lb. 7 oz.
2 cups	whole spelt flour	280 g	10 oz.
1/2 cup	cooked spelt berries, see page 34	75 g	3 oz.
1 tbsp.	quick active dry yeast	11 g	1 tbsp.

Follow the 12-step instructions.

Preheat oven to 350° F.

Spelt Berry Bread - Nutrition Facts (per 45g):

Calories: 100; Total Fat: 1g; Saturated Fat: 0g; Cholesterol: 0mg; Sodium: 95mg; Carbohydrates: 17g; Fibre: 2g; Sugars 1g; Protein: 4g;

Spelt Brown Honey Bread

Spelt Brown Honey Bread

American	Ingredients	Metric	Imperial
2 1/2 cups	hot water, not boiling	600 ml	20 oz.
3 tbsp.	honey	45 ml	3 tbsp.
2 tbsp.	vegetable oil	30 ml	2 tbsp.
2 tsp.	sea salt	2 tsp.	2 tsp.
5 cups 1 tbsp.	white spelt flour	670 g	1 lb. 8 oz.
2 cups	whole spelt flour	280 g	10 oz.
1 tbsp.	quick active dry yeast	11 g	1 tbsp.

Follow the 12-step instructions.

Preheat oven to 350° F.

Spelt Honey Brown Bread - Nutrition Facts (per 45g):

Calories: 100; Total Fat: 1g; Saturated Fat: 0g; Cholesterol: 0mg; Sodium: 95mg; Carbohydrates: 17g; Fibre: 2g; Sugars 1g; Protein: 4g;

White Spelt Bread

❧White Spelt Bread❧

American	Ingredients	Metric	Imperial
2 1/2 cups	hot water, not boiling	600 ml	20 oz.
3 tbsp.	organic cane sugar	50 g	3 tbsp.
2 tbsp.	vegetable oil	30 ml	2 tbsp.
2 tsp.	sea salt	2 tsp.	2 tsp.
7 2/3 cups	white spelt flour	930 g	2 lb.
1 tbsp.	quick active dry yeast	11 g	1 tbsp.

Follow the 12-step instructions.

Preheat oven to 350° F.

White Bread - Nutrition Facts (per 45g):

Calories: 100; Total Fat: 1g; Saturated Fat: 0g; Cholesterol: 0mg; Sodium: 95mg; Carbohydrates: 17g; Fibre: 2g; Sugars 1g; Protein: 4g;

Cooked Spelt Berries

To make a full batch - Good idea to make it the day before

American	Ingredients	Metric	Imperial
2 cups	water	500 ml	16 oz.
1 cup	organic spelt berries/kernels	200 g	7 oz.

Place spelt berries and water in pot, cover and bring to a boil on high heat. Turn heat down to low and let simmer for 1 1/2 hours covered.

Rinse cooked spelt berries in a colander with cold water and refrigerate. You can also freeze left over spelt berries for next time.

Potato Mush

180 grams of raw potatoes cooked in the method below makes 150 grams of potato mush.

Peel potatoes and cut into small (1 1/2 inch) chunks. Place in pot and cover with water. Bring water to a boil and then turn to medium - low and cook uncovered until all cooked. Remove from heat and let sit in pot with water for 10 minutes. Then mash with a potato masher keeping the water in (Do not drain).

Let cool for about half an hour and then use for bread recipes.

Tools And Equipment

Dough Scraper

A dough scraper is the perfect tool for scraping a bowl clean or scraping dough off the counter. They are also very useful for cutting dough when you are making bagels, buns or braided breads like challah. These industrial cooking tools are just beginning to be available in higher end cooking stores.

Whisks

An excellent tool for mixing soft batters, fillings, frostings and yorkshire puddings.

Wooden Spoons

When a dough is too stiff for a whisk, a wooden spoon is best. I have 5 to 8 wooden spoons in my home.

Liquid Measuring Cups

To measure liquid I prefer a clear plastic or glass measuring cup with a pouring spout. They are available in sizes ranging from 1 cup to 8 cups. Place the measuring cup on the counter and add the liquid to the desired measurement.

Dry Measuring Cups

To measure dry ingredients, I prefer a set of nesting metal measuring cups ranging from 1/4 cup to 1 cup. Scoop the dry ingredients with the measuring cup and level off with the flat edge of a knife.

Measuring Spoons

If you can find a set of measuring spoons with 1/8 teaspoon up to 1 tablespoon, purchase it. These are essential for good baking and can be used for measuring small amounts of dry and liquid ingredients.

Mixing Bowls

A nested set of three mixing bowls is a very useful for cookies, cakes, muffins and quick breads, and stainless steel is very versatile. However, for bread dough, nothing beats an 8 to 12 quart stoneware mixing bowl. These are excellent for placing in a warm corner of the kitchen to let your bread dough rise.

Baking Pans

I prefer high quality baking pans as they last for many years. They also conduct heat more efficiently for more even baking. I use an 8 inch loaf pan.

Stand Mixer

There are many high quality stand mixers available in the market today, how- ever, since Spelt flour makes a stiffer dough than wheat flour, a top quality mixer that comes with a dough hook is essential if you want it to last. I have a 5 quart KitchenAid© at home for personal baking.

Personal Notes

www.ingramcontent.com/pod-product-compliance
Lightning Source LLC
Chambersburg PA
CBHW042306150426
43197CB00001B/34